SCHIRMER
PERFORMANCE
EDITIONS

HAL LEONARD PIANO LIBRARY

BEETHOVEN

PIANO SONATA NO. 30

II

T0082013

Edited and Recorded by Robert Taub

Also Available:
BEETHOVEN PIANO SONATAS
edited and recorded by Robert Taub

Volume I, Nos. 1–15
00296632 Book only
00296634 CDs only (5 disc set)

Volume II, Nos. 16–32
00296633 Book only
00296635 CDs only (5 disc set)

On the cover:
The Tree of Crows, 1822 (oil on canvas)
by Caspar David Friedrich
(1774–1840)
© Louvre, Paris, France/Giraudon/The Bridgeman Art Library

ISBN 978-1-4768-1639-5

G. SCHIRMER, Inc.

DISTRIBUTED BY

7777 W. BLUEMOUND RD. P.O. BOX 13819 MILWAUKEE, WI 53213

Copyright © 2012 by G. Schirmer, Inc. (ASCAP) New York, NY
International Copyright Secured. All Rights Reserved.

Warning: Unauthorized reproduction of this publication is
prohibited by Federal law and subject to criminal prosecution.

www.schirmer.com
www.halleonard.com

CONTENTS

PAGE	TRACK	
4		BEETHOVEN AND THE PIANO SONATAS
6		PERFORMANCE NOTES
		Piano Sonata No. 30 in E Major, Opus 109
10	1	Vivace; Adagio espressivo
14	2	Prestissimo
19	3	Gesangvoll, mit innigster Empfindung (Andante molto cantabile ed espressivo)
32		ABOUT THE EDITOR

BEETHOVEN
AND THE PIANO SONATAS

In 1816, Beethoven wrote to his friend and admirer Carl Czerny: "You must forgive a composer who would rather hear his work just as he had written it, however beautifully you played it otherwise." Having lost patience with Czerny's excessive interpolations in the piano part of a performance of Beethoven's *Quintet for Piano and Winds*, Op. 16, Beethoven also addressed the envelope sarcastically to "Herr von Zerni, celebrated virtuoso." On all levels, Beethoven meant what he wrote.

As a composer who bridged the gulf between court and private patronage on one hand (the world of Bach, Handel, Haydn, and Mozart) and on the other hand earning a living based substantially on sales of printed works and/or public perform- ances (the world of Brahms), Beethoven was one of the first composers to become almost obsessively concerned with the accuracy of his published scores. He often bemoaned the seeming unending streams of mistakes. "Fehler—fehler!— Sie sind selbst ein einziger Fehler" ("Mistakes— mistakes!—You yourselves are a unique mistake") he wrote to the august publishing firm of Breitkopf und Härtel in 1811.

It is not surprising, therefore, that toward the end of his life Beethoven twice (1822 and again in 1825) begged his publishers C.F. Peters and Schott to bring out a comprehensive complete edition of his works over which Beethoven himself would have editorial control, and would thus be able to ensure accuracy in all dimensions—notes, pedaling and fingering, expressive notations (dynamics, slurs), and articulations, and even movement headings. This never happened.

Beethoven was also obsessive about his musical sketches that he kept with him throughout his mature life. Desk sketchbooks, pocket sketch- books: thousands of pages reveal his innermost compositional musings, his labored processes of

creativity, the ideas that he abandoned, and the many others—often jumbled together—that he crafted through dint of extraordinary determi- nation, single-minded purpose, and the inspiration of genius into works that endure all exigencies of time and place. In the autograph scores that Beethoven then sent on to publishers, further layers of the creative processes abound. But even these scores might not be the final word in a particular work; there are instances in which Beethoven made textual changes, additions, or deletions by way of letters to publishers, corrections to proofs, and/or post-publication changes to first editions.

We can appreciate the unique qualities of the Beethoven piano sonatas on many different levels. Beethoven's own relationship with these works was fundamentally different from his relationship to his works of other genres. The early sonatas served as vehicles for the young Beethoven as both composer and pianist forging his path in Vienna, the musical capital of Europe at that time. Throughout his compositional lifetime, even when he no longer performed publicly as a pianist, Beethoven used his thirty-two piano sonatas as crucibles for all manner of musical ideas, many of which he later re-crafted—often in a distilled or more rarefied manner—in the sixteen string quartets and the nine symphonies.

The pianoforte was evolving at an enormous rate during the last years of the eighteenth century extending through the first several decades of the nineteenth. As a leading pianist and musical figure of his day, Beethoven was in the vanguard of this technological development. He was not content to confine his often explosive playing to the smaller sonorous capabilities of the instruments he had on hand; similarly, his compositions demanded more from the pianofortes of the day—greater depth of sonority, more subtle levels of keyboard finesse and control, and increased registral range.

These sonatas themselves pushed forward further development and technical innovation from the piano manufacturers.

Motivating many of the sonatas are elements of extraordinary—even revolutionary—musical experimentation extending into domains of form, harmonic development, use of the instrument, and demands placed upon the performer, the piano, and the audience. However, the evolution of these works is not a simple straight line.

I believe that the usual chronological groupings of "early," "middle," and "late" are too superficial for Beethoven's piano sonatas. Since he composed more piano sonatas than substantial works of any other single genre (except songs) and the period of composition of the piano sonatas extends virtually throughout Beethoven's entire creative life, I prefer chronological groupings derived from more specific biographical and stylistic considerations. I delve into greater depth on this and other aspects of the sonatas in my book *Playing the Beethoven Piano Sonatas* (Amadeus Press).

1795–1800: Sonatas Op. 2 no. 1, Op. 2 no. 2, Op. 2 no. 3, Op. 7, Op. 10 no. 1, Op. 10 no. 2, Op. 10 no. 3, Op. 13, Op. 14 no. 1, Op. 14 no. 2, Op. 22, Op. 49 no. 1, Op. 49 no. 2

1800–1802: Sonatas Op. 26, Op. 27 no. 1, Op. 27 no. 2, Op. 28, Op. 31 no. 1, Op. 31 no. 2, Op. 31 no. 3

1804: Sonatas Op. 53, Op. 54, Op. 57

1809: Sonatas Op. 78, Op. 79, Op. 81a

1816–1822: Sonatas Op. 90, Op. 101, Op. 106, Op. 109, Op. 110, Op. 111

From 1804 (post-Heiligenstadt) forward, there were no more multiple sonata opus numbers; each work was assigned its own opus. Beethoven no longer played in public, and his relationship with the sonatas changed subtly.

—*Robert Taub*

PERFORMANCE NOTES

Extracted from *Beethoven: Piano Sonatas Volume II*, edited by Robert Taub.

For the preparation of this edition, I have consulted autograph scores, first editions, and sketchbooks whenever possible. (Complete autograph scores of only twelve of the piano sonatas—plus the autograph of only the first movement of Sonata Op. 81a—have survived.) I have also read Beethoven's letters with particular attention to his many remarks concerning performances of his day and the lists of specific changes/corrections that he sent to publishers. We all know—as did Beethoven—that musical notation is imperfect, but it is the closest representation we have to the artistic ideal of a composer. We strive to represent that ideal as thoroughly and accurately as possible.

Tempo

My recordings of these sonatas are available as companions to the two published volumes. I have also included my suggestions for tempo (metronome markings) for each sonata, at the beginning of each movement.

Fingering

I have included Beethoven's own fingering suggestions. His fingerings—intended not only for himself (in earlier sonatas) but primarily for successive generations of pianists—often reveal intensely musical intentions in their shaping of musical contour and molding of the hands to create specific musical textures. I have added my own fingering suggestions, all of which are aimed at creating meaningful musical constructs. As a general guide, I believe in minimizing hand motions as much as possible, and therefore many of my fingering suggestions are based on the pianist's hands proceeding in a straight line as long as musically viable and physically practicable. I also believe that the pianist can develop senses of tactile feeling for specific musical patterns.

Pedaling

I have also included Beethoven's pedal markings in this edition. These indications are integral parts of the musical fabric. However, since most often no pedal indication is offered, whenever necessary one should use the right pedal—sparingly and subtly—to help achieve legato playing as well as to enhance sonorities.

Ornamentation

My suggestions regarding ornamental turns concern the notion of keeping the contour smooth while providing an expressive musical gesture with an increased sense of forward direction. The actual starting note of a turn depends on the specific context: if it is preceded by the same note (as in Sonata Op. 10 no. 2, second movement, m. 42), then I would suggest that the turn is four notes, starting on the upper neighbor: upper neighbor, main note, lower neighbor, main note.

Sonata in F Major, Opus 10 no. 2:
second movement, m. 42, r.h.

However, if the turn is preceded by another note (as in Sonata Op. 10 no. 2, first movement, m. 38), then the turn could be five notes in total, starting on the main note: main note, upper neighbor, main note, lower neighbor, main note.

Sonata in F Major, Opus 10 no. 2:
first movement, m. 38, r.h.

Whenever Beethoven included an afterbeat (Nachschlag) for a trill, I have included it as well. When he did not, I have not added any.

Footnotes

Footnotes within the musical score offer contextual explanations and alternatives based on earlier representations of the music (first editions, autograph scores) that Beethoven had seen and corrected. In areas where specific markings are visible only in the autograph score, I explain the reasons and context for my choices of musical representation. Other footnotes are intended to clarify ways of playing specific ornaments.

Notes on the Sonata[1]

PIANO SONATA NO. 30 IN E MAJOR, OPUS 109 (1820)

Sonata Op. 109 forges ahead in new ways, with new formal flexibility. The first movement is highly concentrated and compressed, the second—rather than being a slow movement—is extremely fast, and a theme-and-variation movement concludes the work.

The gentle opening of the **Vivace** arises from silence; there are no chords at the beginning, but harmonies accrue as the first note of each group is held through the beat. Rather than starting slightly under tempo and then reaching stride after the first measure or so, I prefer to begin softly and sweetly, but in tempo.

I make the sound of the first of the two notes in each right-hand group slightly heavier than the second, as implied by the quarter-note voicing, but both are sustained throughout the beat. The left-hand groups of two equally voiced sixteenth notes have an implied diminuendo within each group; the second of the two notes is slightly lighter than the first.

I make sure that I hold the pedal until the last sixteenth note in mm. 12–13 as the music of the beginning of the second theme is abstracted into a greater registral span, one that encompassed the full keyboard of Beethoven's instrument. With the *espressivo* marking at the beginning of m. 14, I expand in time as the music climbs ever higher, resuming the normal tempo for this area as the triplets begin to cascade downward.

A crescendo beginning in m. 42 leads to the registrally expansive recapitulation; the beguilingly simple character of the opening theme is now declamatory. When the second theme is repeated (including a *fortissimo* surprise move to C major), it ends in the home key of E major.

In the coda, I make sure the rests in mm. 75–77 are given full value. They are the only silences so far in this movement, and while the harmonies they offset are three pivotal harmonies in the movement, they also create feelings of suspense.

The **Prestissimo** second movement breaks in, *fortissimo*, without a silent pause, before the final chord of the first movement has completely died away. The pulse should be six per bar to avoid playing in two, but the tempo is very fast. To achieve this sort of speed, clarity is necessary. I use well-rounded fingers and only light pedaling. The touch, except when indicated legato by a slur, is lightly detached.

Ironically, the development area of this movement is quiet, although tension simmers beneath the surface. The main line here (m. 70 on) is formed from the bass at the opening of the movement. While the right-hand lines form a canon, intensity is maintained by articulating each note of the left-hand tremolandos. Use light pedal only, and keep a strict pulse of six. The crescendo in mm. 156–157 is challenging, particularly since there is an inclination to rush, but if the pulse is maintained, feelings of surging forward will be more suitably expressed.

In the **Gesangvoll, mit innigster Empfindung (Andante molto cantabile ed espressivo)**, each eight-bar phrase of the theme is repeated, and each time I make sure the left hand is legato in the first three two-part units. As the theme becomes more abstracted in the second variation and the surface pacing increases, clarity of texture is paramount. I use either very light pedal the first time through, or none at all for the interlocking sixteenth-note areas. The third variation, Allegro vivace, is the most brilliant variation of the work. I make the detached eighth notes quite short here. This quick variation leads without pause into the next one, which is specified as being slightly slower than the theme. With the continuous addition of voices, I show the beginning of each with a slight increase of weight of touch. The fifth variation is a fugato; it is here that Beethoven abandoned use of the term "variation" since the form is not followed strictly. I make all the eighth-notes staccato and voice the lines as in a Bach fugue.

1 Excerpted from *Playing the Beethoven Piano Sonatas* by Robert Taub
edited and abridged by Susanne Sheston
© 2002 by Robert Taub
Published by Amadeus Press
Used by permission.

The final variation is the longest. In m. 5, I keep the pulse of the dotted quarter-note equal to that of the quarter-note in m. 4. As the epic trills of the movement begin, the melodic line and the harmonies of the theme are abstracted around trills first in the bass (not so loud as to obscure the top line) and then in the treble. In mm. 25–32 I use the fingering 1–2 for the trill and the fifth finger for the thematic line. Using the pedal as Beethoven suggested in m. 32 creates a *pianissimo* tonic-dominant mist out of which condenses a restatement of the theme, a simple stroke unprecedented in the sonata literature.

A question that inevitably arises for performances of any theme and variations concerns the seams between variations. Should time be taken? If so, how much? Should endings of final phrases be rounded off by slowing down, or remain in tempo?

A subtle hint in the autograph score, one that cannot be gleaned from any printed edition, addresses the issues for Sonata Op. 109. At the end of the theme, Beethoven had initially written *ritardando*. One would assume that this indication applies to the repeated statement of the end of the theme, thus adding to the closure of the theme and separating it somewhat from the first variation. However, after completing the autograph in ink, Beethoven crossed out this *ritardando* in pencil. He then added a *ritardando* and a low E in the bass (also in pencil) in the equivalent place when the theme is restated after the last variation, in the very last measure of the movement.

Since printed scores include no marking here whatsoever, an interpreter might consider a *ritardando* to be in good musical taste at this point. But Beethoven's explicit crossing-out of the *ritardando* at the end of the theme exerts an influence far beyond its immediate locus, as does the addition of the *ritardando* in the final measure of the movement. The interpretive implication of the deletion is that the theme flows seamlessly into the first variation, and the first into the second, and so on. I would not take time between any two variations, nor slow the ending of any until the final measure of the movement, since Beethoven was very explicit about the use of the term *ritardando* and about manipulating the perception of time. The journey through this movement is continuous—and the overall effect of the movement is cumulative—as the music becomes ever more abstract. When the end of the piece is finally attained, the singular *ritardando* in the last measure, the addition of the low E, and a pedal marking with no notated release for the last chord all frame the work in its own essence.

PIANO SONATA NO. 30 IN E MAJOR, Opus 109

Dedicated to Maximiliane Brentano
Sonata in E Major

Ludwig van Beethoven
Opus 109
Composed in 1820

a) As per the autograph. The first edition is Vivace ma non troppo.

Copyright © 2010 by G. Schirmer, Inc. (ASCAP) New York, NY
International Copyright Secured. All Rights Reserved.

b) The autograph contains a bar line at this point (between the G-sharp and A-sharp).

c) The **p** initially at this point in the autograph is crossed out in pencil, with the **f** (also in pencil) added under the chord.

d) The pedal marking in the autograph clearly links these two movements. There is no silence or interruption between them. In addition, the "issimo" of "Prestissimo" was added by Beethoven in the autograph in pencil; see discussion.

e) without tail

f) without tail

Gesangvoll, mit innigster Empfindung (♩ = 60)
Andante molto cantabile ed espressivo

VAR. I
molto espressivo

g) Based on examination of Beethoven's autograph score, I suggest no explicit *ritardando* in this measure (and subsequent last measures of variations as well), thus resulting in a seamless, uninterrupted musical journey through the entire movement. The only true *ritardando* is in the final measure in the recurrence of the theme. See Performance Notes.

VAR. II
leggiermente

VAR. III
allegro vivace

VAR. IV
etwas langsamer, als das Thema
un poco meno andante ciò è un poco più adagio come il tema

piacevole

cresc. — *poco*-*a*-

poco — — — — — — *dim.*

pp

g) In the autograph the fourth eighth note is clearly D-sharp, although the first edition has a B here.

h) **allegro ma non troppo**

h) Beethoven abandons "variation" designation at this point, for the formal structure here is longer than the theme and previous variations; see Performance Notes. "Var. V" is stated in the first edition.

tempo primo del tema ⁱ⁾

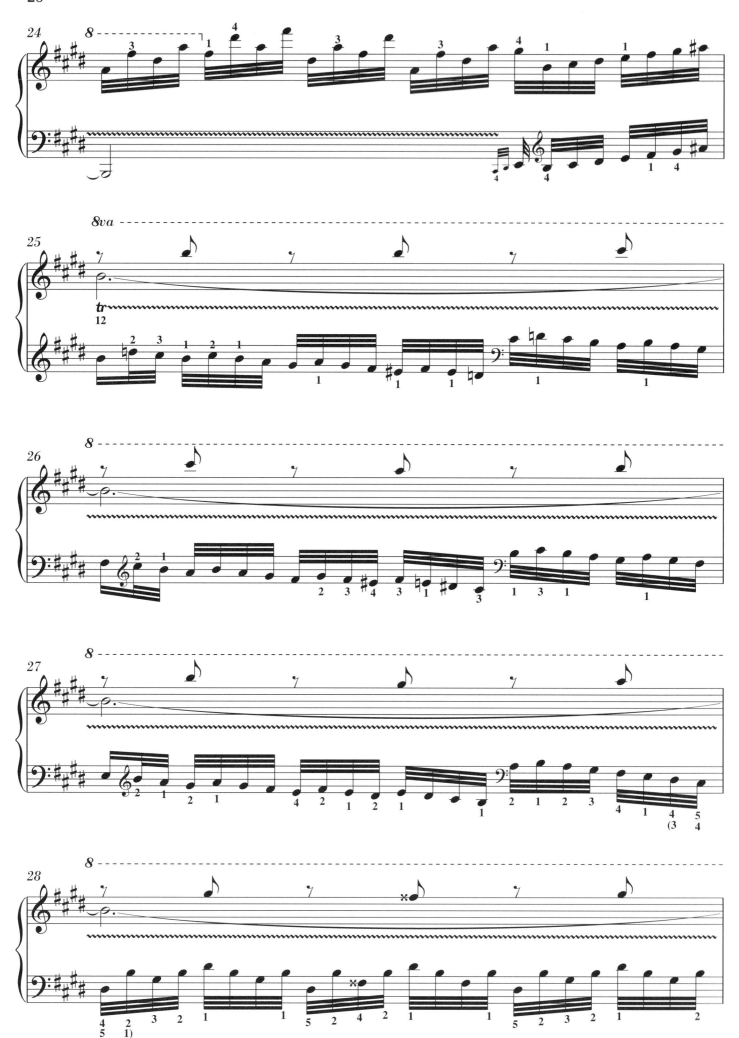

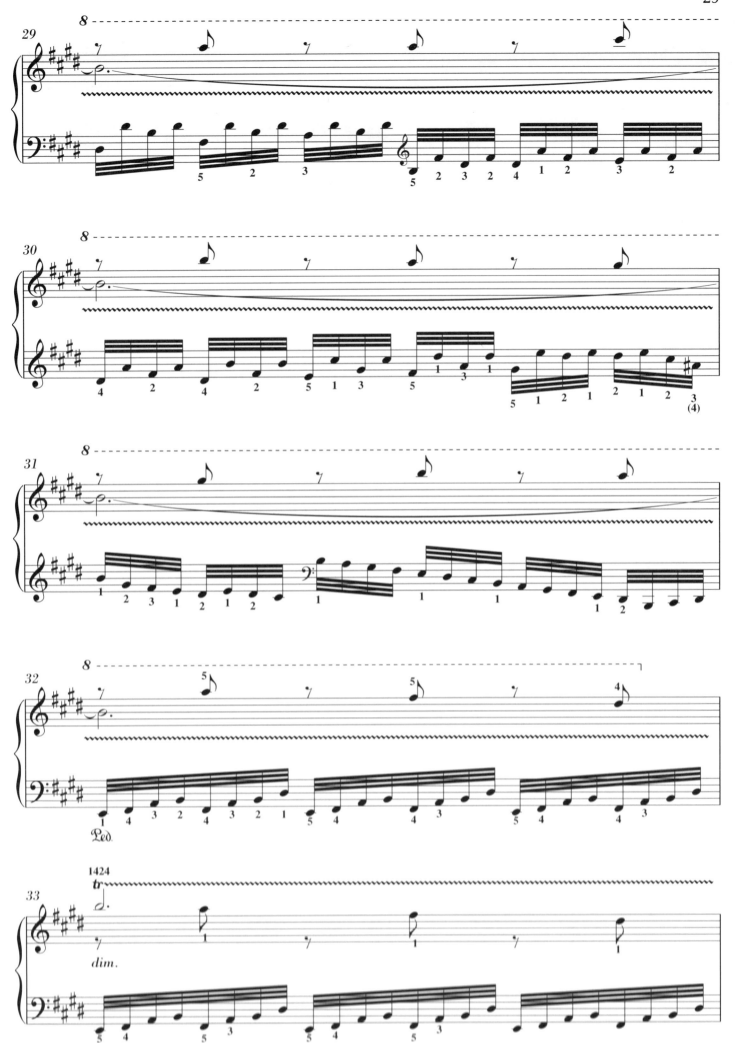

ABOUT THE EDITOR

ROBERT TAUB

From New York's Carnegie Hall to Hong Kong's Cultural Centre to Germany's *avant garde* Zentrum für Kunst und Medientechnologie, Robert Taub is acclaimed internationally. He has performed as soloist with the MET Orchestra in Carnegie Hall, the Boston Symphony Orchestra, BBC Philharmonic, The Philadelphia Orchestra, San Francisco Symphony, Los Angeles Philharmonic, Montreal Symphony, Munich Philharmonic, Orchestra of St. Luke's, Hong Kong Philharmonic, Singapore Symphony, and others.

Robert Taub has performed solo recitals on the Great Performers Series at New York's Lincoln Center and other major series worldwide. He has been featured in international festivals, including the Saratoga Festival, the Lichfield Festival in England, San Francisco's Midsummer Mozart Festival, the Geneva International Summer Festival, among others.

Following the conclusion of his highly celebrated New York series of Beethoven Piano Sonatas, Taub completed a sold-out Beethoven cycle in London at Hampton Court Palace. His recordings of the complete Beethoven Piano Sonatas have been praised throughout the world for their insight, freshness, and emotional involvement. In addition to performing, Robert Taub is an eloquent spokesman for music, giving frequent engaging and informal lectures and pre-concert talks. His book on Beethoven—*Playing the Beethoven Piano Sonatas*—has been published internationally by Amadeus Press.

Taub was featured in a recent PBS television program—*Big Ideas*—that highlighted him playing and discussing Beethoven Piano Sonatas. Filmed during his time as Artist-in-Residence at the Institute for Advanced Study, this program has been broadcast throughout the US on PBS affiliates.

Robert Taub's performances are frequently broadcast on radio networks around the world, including the NPR (Performance Today), Ireland's RTE, and Hong Kong's RTHK. He has also recorded the Sonatas of Scriabin and works of Beethoven, Schumann, Liszt, and Babbitt for Harmonia Mundi, several of which have been selected as "critic's favorites" by *Gramophone, Newsweek, The New York Times, The Washington Post, Ovation,* and *Fanfare*.

Robert Taub is involved with contemporary music as well as the established literature, premiering piano concertos by Milton Babbitt (MET Orchestra, James Levine) and Mel Powell (Los Angeles Philharmonic), and making the first recordings of the Persichetti Piano Concerto (Philadelphia Orchestra, Charles Dutoit) and Sessions Piano Concerto. He has premiered six works of Milton Babbitt (solo piano, chamber music, Second Piano Concerto). Taub has also collaborated with several 21st-century composers, including Jonathan Dawe (USA), David Bessell (UK), and Ludger Brümmer (Germany) performing their works in America and Europe.

Taub is a Phi Beta Kappa graduate of Princeton where he was a University Scholar. As a Danforth Fellow he completed his doctoral degree at The Juilliard School where he received the highest award in piano. Taub has served as Artist-in-Residence at Harvard University, at UC Davis, as well as at the Institute for Advanced Study. He has led music forums at Oxford and Cambridge Universities and The Juilliard School. Taub has also been Visiting Professor at Princeton University and at Kingston University (UK).